SNOWSCAPE WITH SIGNATURE

ABDUR-RAHMAN SLADE HOPKINSON

SNOWSCAPE WITH SIGNATURE
poems, 1952 - 1992

PEEPAL TREE

First published in Great Britain in 1993
Peepal Tree Books
17 King's Avenue
Leeds LS6 1QS
England

ISBN 0 948833 74 2

ACKNOWLEDGEMENTS

Some of the poems published in this collection have appeared previously in the following journals and anthologies: *Bim, Caribbean Quarterly, New World Monthly, Savacou, Anansesem, A Shapely Fire, Breaklight, Caribbean Voices, Commonwealth Poetry Today, Heinemann Book of Caribbean Poetry, The Penguin Book of Caribbean Verse,* and *Voiceprint*.

CONTENTS

IV

INTRODUCTION

In 1954-5, my first year at the University College of the West Indies, Mona, Slade Hopkinson was one of the senior students. He was also one of the most memorable, from time to time declaiming Shakespeare roles from a Chancellor Hall balcony at two o'clock in the morning. He was a member of an elite group of West Indian artist-intellectuals (including Derek Walcott) — actors, playwrights, directors, painters, poets, critics, conversationalists — that helped create the high style much admired in those days. He was already a remarkable actor. Some details of his Lear — his processional entrance as decrepit majesty, head tilted at a petulant angle; his visceral howl of suffering in the storm — are remembered still.

'Inward, downward was always the way.' Slade was already a serious poet — *The Four and other poems* was published in Barbados in 1954, and he was included in Edna Manley's 1956 *Focus*, published in Jamaica. Born in Guyana in 1934, he was educated there and in Barbados (at Harrison College) and Jamaica (the UCWI). As a schoolmaster, journalist, university lecturer, information officer, he has lived and worked in and for various territories of the Caribbean — he long ago 'began/ A game and career of hopscotch round the islands'. His wife, Freda, is Jamaican. He and his family moved to Canada in 1977 and they now reside in Toronto. In *Snowscape with Signature* there are poems explicitly set in Jamaica, Barbados, Trinidad,

Guyana or elsewhere, including North America.

At the back of the book, brief notes gloss some Caribbean and other references essential to understanding of the poems: not only *baakoo, stellings, agouti, congeree*, but also Maud Gonne, O. Henry, J.M.W. Turner and so on. (The persona is often someone conscious of — and ironic about — colonial heritage, as in 'Rain Over St. Augustine', 'I thought of Turner, for I am educated'). But for many readers, perhaps, the necessary notes are those that help us with Muslim allusions. Slade became a Muslim in 1964. He put out as parallel collections (Georgetown: Ministry of Education and Social Development, 1976) *The Madwoman of Papine* by Slade Hopkinson and *The Friend* by Abdur-Rahman, his Muslim name.

It is probably useful also to know that, because of a serious kidney problem, he has for many years been on dialysis. His condition colours some of the work, and seems central to poems such as 'Whirlpool' and 'Traffic Jam in Sickness' ('dead/ tired waiting for your vivacity/ to come back from vacation...'). Like many other poets, he monitors perception, he contemplates the ravages of time, he writes of nature, art, love, death, not often dealt with singly. 'The year is dying./ My time is dying./ What have I planted, Lord?' He deals corrosively with social indifference (as in 'The Madwoman of Papine'), wasteful violence (as in 'The Chord' where 'Anthurium lilies of blood, gristle, bone/ Bloom on the damp, newspapered walls of home'), conflicts of race and politics. He is wittily alert to paradox. 'I pretend belief in what I assume I see.' Writing occasionally in Creole, but most often in standard English, he achieves 'A poised yet individual tone' — as, for example, movingly, in one of my favourites, 'An Oath'. Perhaps his most distinctive contribution to West Indian poetry, however, is in his religious poems, including 'Neither Fog nor Flight', 'In One Swift Year' and 'Ahad' which includes these lines of submission to the source:

I am a shade
Cast by Your shadow
The sweetest of metres
Is drummed by Your name.

('Ahad')

I welcome *Snowscape with Signature*, Abdur-Rahman Slade Hopkinson's most substantial collection.

Mervyn Morris

I

THESE POEMS ARE...:

a gift to my dead mother, to my dead father,
and to my cousin, the poet, Martin Carter,
and to some other few:
a hoard secreted in a public place.
Such confidences may
be bound in book and sport a public face,
and yet they will
be understood as confidences still
by her
and him
and you.

INTRO

No effort of perception I have made
    Has ever helped me touch reality.
Gaping long at this play as it is played,
    I pretend belief in what I assume I see.
Buildings, landscapes with figures, seem a film,
    Transparent, flat, with an arbitrary frame.
The silence in my head can overwhelm
    Them, and reduce dense substance to pure name.
And so I now investigate my loves,
    And note the fluid images congeal-
ing on each patient page, till each page proves
    That the host to real griefs must himself be real.
And I, ex-slave from sugar's golden times,
Choose my own irons; these free, linked English rhymes.

II

THE MADWOMAN OF PAPINE

Two cartoons with captions

(1)

Four years ago,
in this knot of a village north of the university,
she was in residence
where a triangle of grass gathered the mountain road,
looped it once, and tossed it to Kingston,
where grampus buses, cycling students,
duppies of dust and ululations in light
vortexed around her.
Ritualist, she tried to reduce the world,
sketching her violent diagrams
against a wall of mountains which her stare made totter.
Her rhythmic ideas detonated into gestures.
She would jab her knee into the groin of the air,
fling her sharp instep at the fluttering sky,
revise perspectives with the hooks of her fingers,
and butt blood from the teeth of God.

She cooked and ate anything. But, being so often busy,
she hardly ever cooked or ate.

What of her history?
These are the latitudes of the ex-colonised,
of degradation still unmollified,
imported managers, styles in art,
second-hand subsistence of the spirit,
the habit of waste,
mayhem committed on the personality,
and everywhere the wrecked or scuttled mind.

Scholars, more brilliant than I could hope to be,
advised that if I valued poetry,
I should eschew all sociology.
Who could make anything of a pauper lunatic
modelling one mildewed dress from year to year?
Scarecrow, just sane enough occasionally
to pick up filth and toast it on a brick,
and then renew
the comic mime of her despair.

Clearly something was very wrong with her
as subject. Pedestrian. Too limited
for lyric literature.
I went away for four years. Then returned.

(2)

One loaf now costs what two loaves used to.
The madwoman has crossed the road
and gone behind the shops
nearer the university,
oriens ex occidente lux,
the light of scholars rising in the west.
She wears the same perennial dress,
now black as any graduate's gown,
but stands in placid anguish now,
perfects her introverted trance
with hanging arms, still feet,
chin on breast, forehead parallel
to the eroded, indifferent earth,
merely an invisible old woman,

extremist votary at an interior altar,
repeatedly rinsing along her tongue
a kind of invocation, whispered, verbless:

'O
Rass Rass Rass
in the highest.'

DEATH IS NOT THE UNDISCOVERED COUNTRY

Death is not the undiscovered country;
Death is right here. You have walked these cities,
Walked them in the day, on casual business,
Walked them at night, and then you remembered:
The dead night. Death is not undiscovered.
Walking and walking when it was lonely,
And the darkness lent you its impersonality,
Walked by the wharves and passed by the seaboard,
Looked at the wharf boards sprinkled with fish scales,
Seen the bananas, flattened, half-rotten,
The dirty rags, and the piles of wet sugar.
Then you remembered the shining stevedores,
At lunch time their cracked teeth tied with mango threads,
And under the brick wall the pungent urine,
And you remembered their look of impersonality,
The scuffle for a living, the mechanical death.
In the morning you never thought about them.
After the day walk you remembered only the heat.
And you know you will see them again tomorrow.

Remember tomorrow
    Death too keeps time,
The clockwork heartbeats
    Recur like rhyme.
These are the true dead,
    The truly forgotten,
Their bodies a nausea,—
    With routine sweat rotten.

THE MIGHTY INTRIGUER, CALYPSONIAN, SINGS HIS ANTICIPATION OF THE COMING CARNIVAL

(*a song from a play*)

Last month was me last pay day,
I ain't go' see no more pay,
Me shirt is just rip and fray,
I hungry the livelong day,
A dollar won't even stray
Across old Intriguer way.
                    What wrong?
The boss tell me wend me way,
The boss tell me wend me way.

But me carnival money
    Salted away.
I bank for the fancy
    Mas' I go' play.
Ballade go' tickle
    The high and the low;
Intriguer go' make it
    New in calypso.

Small farmers, they making moan,
They wasting their sweat and brawn.
Cassava won't grow 'pon stone,
Drought suck the land dry as bone.
Alice touch me for a loan,
Intriguer lie back and groan,
                    And she?
Pick up petticoat and gone,
Pick up petticoat and gone.

Don't ask me from where I
        Go' get me next pay;
But me carnival coppers
        Salted away.
Ballade go' tickle
        The high and the low;
Intriguer go' make it
        Brand new in calypso.

HAM IN EXILE

(*On a white limestone bust of a negro, immediate ancestor and cousin of the black man*)

(1)

Displaced Ham, your sculptor's choice
Of limestone tells with irony
(More truly than if he had used
Descriptive, literal ebony)

The double, long bewilderment
Of a soul exiled and composite:
Black, shame-faced, sick with self-contempt
Reshapes itself in spiritual white.

(2)

Europe invents. In her western lands,
Created with three caravels,
Arguments of whip and Cross
Convince, convert brute infidels.

A scorpion sun crawls in the sky
Over plantation mounds and furrows.
Deployed around great-houses rise
Phalanxes of canes in arrow.

(3)

But this is not the story's end:
Expedient morals manumit
Hands, but can't do the same for mind,
Bleached in the school that tutored it.

(4)

The Mother Country's tutelage,
    Her skills and science guarantee
Assuagement of her pupil's rage,
    Unoverseered conformity.

Exile, which is both to and from,
    Withers the severed root of merit.
A poised yet individual tone
    Eludes the language you inherit.

Useless to make excuse, from hurt,
    For the present history has arranged
For you, who cannot now revert
    To origins from which you've changed.

No variants of posture, twang,
    Talent, or shekel-earning task
Erase this old dilemma, traced
    On your off-white mental mask.

Note: on every exile's face
    The pupil's self-apology,
Which your sculptor's limestone choice
    Derides with literal irony.

'RETOUR AU PAYS NATAL', 1963

For Martin Carter

The undercarriage gropes
Downward with our intention and our plane's.
As yet I can read no welcome
In the cursive hand of rivers on their green page.

Easy in the next seat Freda my wife
Grins at my sweat-flecked brow and explaining finger,
Croons, 'Hush, Nalo,' soothing our daughter's alarm
At the plunging of our aerial roller-coaster.

Sixteen years since I began
A game and career of hopscotch round the islands ...
Look! Rivers, forests still in place! What did I expect?
My country's features age less obviously than mine.

Wheels grip the runway. The plane
Takes its weight, and ours, off its wings ...
Swings toward the timber terminal building (timber enough
For building in my country) ... Engines stutter out ...

Measuring my steps, I tremble down the gangway.
Furtively I place palm on ground, then touch palm to my lips,
Ashamed of my rather more theatrical impulse.
My education has been in the Proprieties.

Later in the lounge my cousin Martin Carter,
Haranguing friends, elbow hooking a bottle,
Turns, squints, straightens, then heaves at me
An embrace as huge as all our forests.

Freda and Nalo instantly at home,
Even among West Indian writers:
(Where
Are the usual glib, cosmopolitan airs?)

In spite of sixteen years
I watch and deeply read
The Demerara's cursive hand on its green page.

THE SELF-FULFILMENT OF BIG RIVERS

Men of my time and country stand rebuked by
The self-fulfilment of big rivers. Constrictions caused
By cataracts, for instance, or the unrusting iron
Of fallen greenheart trunks, cannot be considered
Lenders of mettle to these live waters.
Mettle is the prime property of these waters —
And joy, divine hurdler over boulders, shoals,
The slabbed, butting foreheads of waterfalls,
Mere petty slate or granite interruptions.

Beyond the savannahs, in the Sierra Acarai,
The thundering cloudfist of the arm of God
Flings rain like knives, slicing the Essequibo
Into the landscape loaved with mountains. Born
Are the desire and career of the river.
Its prodigality awes. It permits itself
Intricate whorls, backwashings, forthright leaps,
Fluent extravaganzas in umber and ochre.
Primness is the enemy of beauty. Determination
Is tight, strenuous only. But this river
Follows the compass of its need, ignoring
The congregations of the suppliant trees,
The coiled, glutted greed of anacondas,
Macaws and toucans with their shrieks and rainbows,
The poisonous gravel of insects, raping mines,
Protesting islands, waddling steamers, punts,
The serviceable, stilted wharves and *stellings*,
Longing for its estuary.

In the capital,
A jewel on the demure Demerara,
The cultured men of my time watch cultured fountains,

Mechanically trained, derive their dances;
Tamers of water and imagination,
Trying to discount the river.

My country offers other instances
Of energy: men crippled in the intellect,
Who serve their cretinous, gunpowdered lusts,
Raging with dum-dum glance and cutlass teeth.
But you are no image of them:
Neither like *auntieman* nor racist beast,
Your main and tributary waters branched
But homogeneous, like all human blood,
My Essequibo!

Blood will be paid in full for blood, when finally
Holy imagination dies, and intellect
Collapses, impaled on its splintered crutches.

Let me not think of that.

                                        Look! Where the river
Stacks its alluvial beach, the boys are managing
The rainbow resurrections of their kites
In the blue estuary of the Trades.

GUYANA: FREEDOM YEAR

(*NOTE: In the year 1962, all letters sent out by government departments in the then colony of British Guiana were stamped with the slogan 'Freedom Year', in anticipation of the achievement of independence. That year there were political riots and arson in many parts of the country, and the Indians and the Africans, who together constitute the majority of the population, were more hostile to each other than ever before. That year, too, the government announced that the colony, after achieving its freedom, would be renamed Guyana. 'Independence', whatever that was intended to mean, whatever different interests intended or did not intend to make it mean, was granted on May 26, 1966).*

Says official strategy:
'This year each one shall be free',—
Fratricide and poet too,
Peasant and incendiary.

December vents the thunderstorm:
So paddy thrives, and scorpion.
Where the creek slops curdling bile
The railway bridge thrusts down its piles
Shading the eggs of crocodiles.

Note that the river bed conceals
Nuggets, and spawn of deadly eels.
Note too: the selfsame land can feed
The agouti, and the centipede.

In a guest house once at Bartica
In the slipper at my father's foot,
Each hair bristling from its root,
Hid the starred tarantula.

Note well: across the country's face,
Mocking hypocrite pose and creed,
Enmities of blood and race
Branch like rivers, and disgrace
Each father's seed.

THE JAGUAR AND THE THEORIST OF NÉGRITUDE

The Nigerian poet Wole Soyinka, apropos of the literary movement known as négritude, has said somewhere that a tiger does not go about proclaiming its tigritude: it just pounces.

The jungle, grown impatient with us all,
Has marched on military feet,
Has assaulted the rice and sugar coastland,
Checkerboard of historical habit.
The jungle's retribution
Has invaded the capital.
In every street, branched giants have uprooted houses.
Monkeys with green faces and critical eyes
Open doors or climb into windows.
Terrible is their barking laughter.

Contrivances of our desperate spirit fail.
The sham we thought was our reality boils,
Evaporates, is gone, not even a fume
Remains. Inside each hollow skull
Something rattles, — perhaps a knuckle
Of the dead, still weeping man, that, as he rubbed
The dusty trickle of his tears, became unhinged
And fell behind the absence of his eyes.
Ant-bears scribble with their snouts and tongues
Daintily on the infested skin of corpses.
Fleshy flowers, beating like live hearts,
Decorate the starkness of our pavements.
Troops of vipers move deployed, my love.
Essential horror has occurred, my love.

In the middle of an important street
An inventor of the black man's soul lies dead.

His fingers clutch neither machete nor bomb,
But an anguished book he wrote, — published in England.

O jaguar, lady, muse, teacher, it was you
Who banged your jaws into his throat, then ripped.

WATERMELONS

(*For a guerrillera*)

Yes. This is — approximately — a watermelon,
Anaemic colour, unambitious size,
Rind ribbed with greyish green and greenish grey,
Seeds maggot-white, a few brown, slotted in
To carry on their northern generation
In these precise and stingy growing seasons,
Abruptly started, as abruptly finished.
Split into quarters, saran-wrapped, you see it
On the supermarket's chilled shelf cringe and sulk.

In our hot, showery, gold-lit latitudes
The circular growing season is forever.
There is a child-like daemon of the vine,
Balloon-cheeked like the bebop trumpeter,
Who claps his lips to the stalks, and blows, and shapes,
With sweetest-dripping flesh instead of breath,
Miles-Davis-notes of melons, heavy, full.
Gun-metal-green rind lapped round blood-red flesh,
Each stamps a deep dent in its hill and bed.
In Trinidad at the highway's edge you see them
Packed high in pyramids, like cannon shot.
They seem to tilt the island with their bulk.

And you, magnolia of our latitudes,
Pink-starred in season, guerrilla-green in season,
Raising such dizzy questions in men's hearts
That they astound themselves with love of you —
Magnolia stellata, can you tell why our soils,
That grow such melons, cannot keep our people?
Why is that our writers, chained to our
Epic, demeaning tragedies of race,
(Harvest of language fruitfully replanted)

Fuss at the edge of our rich human theme?
Why are the arsenals full, while our starved children,
Dozing on bloated guts, start at their dream?

THE CHORD

(*For R.H.*)

God knows, that's too much terror for your years.
You tell so gamely of the children, dead —
Friends, playmates, neighbours — shot, not on the street,
But indoors, wasted on the cowardly night.
Anthurium lilies of blood, gristle, bone
Bloom on the damp, newspapered walls of home,
A jolly pattern for the children's room.
You do not mention the slack arithmetic
Of undifferentiating machine guns
That, shifting, might have numbered you as well.
The tolling bells alarm
Yet one more on our rope of paradises
Strung at the throat of stunned America.
Predictable, like our tourist-brochure sun,
We see the patterned sequence run
Of old imperial new fraternal war —
History, as repetitious as a gun.

What justice is there for the children — dead?
'None none none none'
Coughs the staccato gun.

Then label every infant hearse,
Every coffin, with a verse:
A verse, the poet's futile strength and rage.
Link, little poetess, word to singing word.

Each verse excites the Caribbean pattern.
Cued by your grieving, five
Adopted tongues, five voices cross our sea:
They're scored together in one shuddering chord.

III

GOING FOR A DRIVE

Driving outward,— to the airport, let us say,—
    Seems in each island longer than the return.
Mnemonic details punctuate the way:
    Splayed tree, delicate fern,

Landspit, rickety, abandoned trash hut,
    Drifts of white gaulins powdering the grass,
Canefields on fire, broadcasting waves of soot ...
    And potholes, potholes ... impasse after impasse ...

Still, finally there. Pinned to your blouse, fragrant fern.
    We sit and order drinks. The irrelevant crowd
Of passengers bickers, scribbles. Palm to palm we burn,
    Forehead to forehead bowed.

Loved details on love's outward journey. And then?
    Abrupt return to before-love, let us say.
Are you yet, ghost, with me? Did you chill, quick heart, in a
    trice?
    Or from the tarmac fly away?

AN OATH

(*For F.H.*)

Now at this altar I swear,
Altar rubbled by time,
But unwilted in my hopes,
Weeds on an unknown sea,
With my crumb of sincerity,
At the start of the shaky year,
My feet gummed in slime
And my heart in the mouth of fear.

From your bruised simplicity hear
Me, as each day repeats
The eternal sun and my oath
Bright as recurring grace:

If ever with intent I hurt
Or abuse the faith of your love
(Which quietly defeats
All disadvantages)
May death, which is my due
In any case, at once
Eradicate, nullify
(This is no idle breath)
Me and any fruit
Of my still optimist mind

And the irreversible rust
Seize me.

BAAKOO

Me, ghoul, frantic, cramped and bottled,
From this side of the inferno please permit me
To cable you, O shamelessly, for help.
I hanged myself, for bleak compassion's sake,
Long years ago.   Garrotted.   Throttled.

I now decide, belatedly, to live.

You who have touched me, will you help me wake?

GHOST

No woman there.
Just I. And love. An abstract need. A hint.
No object to that love.
Then suddenly, you. Of mental stuff. Of air.
Translucent skin of peanut-butter tint.
The face a pert triangle. And, above,
Intangible, black, flouncing hair.

No body there,
But mine. Just mine. Now, this you. Mere idea
Condensing in my head.
A turbulence of wishes in the air.
An eddy of honey light. What am I now to say,
Or do? Lie silent on my single bed,
Frightened by luck, and stare.

O ghost, my validator! Live
Forever in your land of unpossession,
Essence of me, and yet beyond the mesh
Of contract, every negative
Dead formula and withering obligation.
Do not descend to flesh,
For you, or I, may grow acquisitive.
Do not descend.
                    Not yet
                              Not yet ...
                                        And yet ...

SEASONS

Snow-sheeted rigor mortis of the year
North of hot Cancer;
But within-heart the moon shines always clear.
Stiff sap must thaw.

Sharp, desiccating sun-stroke in July
Near the equator;
The moon shines clear.
Rain will end drought.

The coded, strict vocabulary of love
Echoes the shifting seasons:
Weathers in the air above
Choke or elate the heart.

Teach my four-season-tutored mind to cope
With my own love and weathers.
Be my verse unbaffled
When overseer sun flogs
Or when flood seasons lour.
Make me familiar
With lady-of-the-night, crazing lovers,
And so familiar sunflower.

AT THE LOOKOUT

(*From a lost short story. The character who writes this poem is a pathetic and comic young man who can express himself only on paper*).

Stars hang below us also. Port of Spain:
    Lamp-constellations mimicking the sky.
    (Impersonal paper can't embarrass; try —
Dear God, her grace deserves it — try to be plain).

You sensitize my nerves. I feel the whorl and grain
    Of fingertips. Your eyes scribble the list
    Of my evasions on the thinning mist.
The moon whitewashes us with milky rain.

(I fail to write it now, dear, just as I failed
    To say it then, but try, as then I tried
        To chain the moment, with time running out).
    I cup your face in my hands. I hug your side.

(Forgive my reticence. Your clear gaze impaled
        My spirit. Someone I do too little about).

TERRIBLE MOON

I live in terror of her
Who in her tyranny
Often deserts, never releases, me.

THE WAY BACK

(*The poet-actor ruminates*)

To pick the way
Back to your first moon-smitten joy in her,
After long years of carnival play,
Seduction by the patter
Of manicured hands in the theatre ...

Not that you wish
To disown, now, your jumbie mask or stage.
Many a hidden rage or joy
Has flamed at your formal, acted joy or rage.
But the carnival's just paper, the play's scenery cloth,
Applauding hands are only scented skin,
And to some peeping souls
Their word-and-gesture-induced merriment or terror
Are temporary wrinkles on the face,
Symptoms of mere theatre.
                But you recall the white, hair-raising moon
                In the sky's dish,
                And a haunted boy scribbling on a haunted page.

Are you confined, at thirty-three,
To the actor's staged immodesty
And the mas' player's flippancy?

Patience. Take heart.
Manicured hands clap next to callused hands.
The show is real, though dressed in cloth and paper,
And a real jumbie haunts the theatre.
Inward, downward was always the way.
And some will laugh, or hack, themselves to death
Because of a right rhythm on your breath.

Still,
Have you become a man of heretic will?
Are stage and costume outlawed by her laws?

After the curtain call, the final blackout,
Enter the midnight, turning inward, downward,
Forget applauding hands, and contemplate
The different devotion due to her.

Shun prospects of neither love nor error
Felt honestly or honestly made, but look
Askance at formal faiths, their strict squint-vision.

Take with detachment every task and salary
Except the affliction of her gift of grace
Whose favour keeps full the rivers of the mind,
Whose kind was once exclusively your kind.

ON THE BEACH IN ANOTHER ISLAND

Winds rip across the Atlantic, and I weep,
Stung by their slap. Or are my tears a clue
To my folly all these days and wind-ripped days
When my heart wastes itself with missing you?
I stare across the Atlantic's rumpled sheet,
And bide my time, and follow my aimless feet.

TWO GALLEONS

'*Muse, you have bitten through my fool's finger*'.
Robert Graves

Maud Gonne? To me? You, without violence;
Vanity masking prudent innocence;
Heart-wrecker, as you think you see yourself;
Your own heart, like a trinket, left on a shelf
For him to come and take it down. Safe, safe;
If shipwrecked pride will let him still be brave,
Again his galleon heart may be your trinket box.

Tell yourself so. But each tear-moistened lid,
Halving to wistfulness an eye
Perfect before, except for want of that,
To my tear-moistening tenderness unlocks
A cache: one jewelled mirror. Blink, blink hard;
Latch fast those lids. Adjust the mask. Don't bare
That image in your damp, droop-lidded stare:
My shattered, salvaged galleon towed to your dockyard.

ORANGES

Tablets for human problems. A man can come
To love them; what is funnier,
To desire them, as a man in healthy love
Desires the woman he loves. Worst of all, after
The comic delirium tremens of love and desire,
A man can come
To deserve them, just as every man deserves,
With mathematical justice, the woman he has chosen.

I steer the cymbals of my car
That stutters for want of gas, into a station.
Sleep failing to erase his astonishment,
The attendant guides me with as dainty care
As if I were taxi-ing a jumbo jet to its halt.
His precision dignifies my rattletrap.
Unable to make myself feel thanks, I watch him
From eyes I hope are as dead as trapped smoke.
Self-pity entitles me to be very tired.
Officious compassion of the tablet bottle
Offers itself from the ledge above the dashboard.
I take, out of self-pity, one, and again one,
Then study the man, marvelling himself out of sleep,
Injecting fuel into my dry gas tank.
('So glad my car affords you such amusement').

Pain of the loss of what I never had
Stabs me with chemical efficiency.
In spite of that, I feel
Detached enough to long for my desk and this poem,
For you have entered the foreground of my mind,
(As if you ever leave it)
And I sit, fatigued with uphill exaltation.

Entering the foreground of my mind, you bring,
Absent though you physically are,
The scent of oranges and rain on hill slopes.

Pebbles of orange, green and yellow shake
In the shac-shac of my fist.
Dance music floods my memory.
Percussions deeper in the mind
Leave every fête behind.
I who have held you in uncertain arms,
Eyes clenched against the torture of the moon,
Was blind, was therefore blind.

Legitimately we may have
Whatever tablet will sedate our need.
A pharmacist cures our humanity,
The heart's greed.

I pitch the bottle, smashing it on the pavement.
And orange, green and yellow tablets change
To green and yellow oranges on hill slopes
Powdered with cloud, drummed on by musical rain.

I do not need a pebble on my tongue
To make me clearly speak.
I hold the scent of orange leaf and rind,
Contented, in my smitten mind.
The attendant lifts his hand and steps aside.
Percussive memories of rain
Help me to ride
Calmly, O calmly now,
The downhill undulations of my pain.

MANTRAM

Blood, like an earthquake, rocks my mortal ground.
    I love you, for I cannot wake alone.
Murmuring in dream this mantram, I astound
    The drowsiness of mind, heart, sinew, bone.

WHIRLPOOL

He felt it coming on him once again,
Wave after hammering wave of his unreason.
Midnight migraine. Vision, hearing, images
Cross-linked, so that the spasms of his heart
Squeezed his brain like a rubber ball. Or, driving,
He (and every other driver) seemed to fly
Along a street *up there*, while far below him,
The blue sky hung, and swung, a censer smoking
With incense at high mass; for 'work is prayer',
Laborare est orare,
So the quotation said, as irrelevant
As the No Entry sign he had confronted.

Her imagined eyes beside him, her damp eyes,
(Always her eyes) registered, then flashed sternly:
'You cannot let it happen now. Or ever again.
For you are in my hands now, I in yours,
Cross-linked as ever, ever.' Rhythmic migraine
Ebbed to the rhythm of her words.
'We are cross-linked by the same boring threats,
Irrelevant temptations, and the same
Whirlpool of universal downwardness,
Against which we link hands and counter-twist,
Climbing the whirlpool's negative screw.

Turn the car.

There are other ways. Don't let No Entry stop
Us in the ways we planned. Dear, if you do,
You give in to the whirlpool, and we drop.'

SANITY

Who would debate
    The sky's blue?
Nor am I sane
    Save in you.

Amateurs prevail in
    These latitudes.
O help steady my mind, tossed
    Through howling feuds

With those who destroy
    The word's root in love;
With myself, fatigued
    From the patience of love.

'Only total risk
    Can perfect love or art.'
Thus you sternly bring peace
    To my appalled heart.

No, I do not debate
    The sky's blue,
But entrust my frail reason
    To you.

A SONG FOR YOU AT HISTORY'S TURNING

(*Trinidad, 1971, at the time of the black power riots*).

'Now days are dragon-ridden, the nightmare
Rides upon sleep ...'

W.B. Yeats

Soldiers clog the thoroughfares,
Armed citizens huddle in the hills.

Keep, by your beauty, me entranced,
So I desire perfection always
In everything I will to do,
And do by my (through only you)
Perfected will. So every act,
Each future that I step into
Aims at its end to merit you,
A benediction at your hands,
And when I fail I start again.

Violent necessity
Perhaps will detonate our shame
And detonate our cowardice:
Modes of defensive cowardice
And the self-revenge of shame.

A footnote at my page's foot
Says that the juice of cane is bitter—
Stale-bitter as man's livelong sweat.

Another footnote counterpoints
'The whip of sugar cane's a cliche;
Hatred and vengeance are absurd.'
'As human,' says the mirror-writing
Reflected from the second note,

'As human as my genius,
Divine, beyond my anxious will,
That flares each image in my mind,
And flares my unmalicious rage.'

If such quarrel with myself
May be called a song for you,
(For there's no I that is not you)
I sing for you at history's turning,
And do not think it will be pretty.
No, love, it is the pity of
Necessity, as perfect as
The simple sentence of your smile,
And the amber echoes of your eyes.
I pity the events of time
With my ego's pointless pity,
And with those very tears I bless
The excellence you turn me to,
And weep my thanks that you should be,
As blades of cane leaves turn to metal,
Cane juice foams bitter, and our brothers
Grasp their slick machetes in sleep.

REIGN OF TERROR, 1970: A NIGHTMARE

I cry to you for help. But who are you?
    No woman's here. Chair empty. Empty bed.
A spendthrift's tattered sheets soaked through and through
    With sweat. A grey mosquito net overhead.

My eyelids close. Or do they? On the screen
    Of lid, or net, projected from my brain
Beam racing images of terror. Clean
    Bullet holes through my fainting flesh. No pain.

Centred in fever's vertigo, I burn
    With need to know you, half-imagined love.
Is no one here to wake me? None to turn
    This reeling film of nightmare soldiers off?

Nightmares of black, sardonic soldiers fly
As I create my love, to whom I cry.

FLYING LIGHT

(For F.H.)

The hours each leap higher towards the zenith of noon
    Like a gradated range of skyscrapers.
In my final New York hotel room
    Frayed, middle-aged shirts, papers,

Shoes with mileage-bevelled heels on the rack,
Centuries of poetry proliferating in paperback,
    A travelling student's year of accumulations,—
Well, I must pack.

Outside, a stinging loop of heat
    Traps the city's rust-coloured, industrial breath.
Lungs discover cigarettes are unnecessary
    For a cancerous death.

A finger on the abacus of my mind
    Numbers these modern, still-strange images.
Nuclear formulas, like clouds of supersonic birds,
    Condense abruptly on the trees.

Damn my rampant, hungover imagination,
    Dam this river of metaphors in spate.
Packing is the present imposition,—
    The inevitable overweight.

Dump the trash. These reproductions dilute Van Gogh.
    Such anaemias for purples, O, such timorous greens!
And what use are all these evanescent essays
    Secreted in precious, evanescent magazines?

I hide two pairs of disintegrating shoes
    On the topmost shelf in a room-high closet,
Gather an armful of academic notes
    And in the wastebasket bank a long-term deposit.

Time for home.
    High time to fly.
A poet grounded
    By property?

Laughable! So, sky time!
    My darling, my home, I hear you laugh and approve.
May I shed, always shed, fly light, nimble
    As verse, as love.

ORIGAMI

(*For Tami Fugimoto*)

A frog, gem-green — like the Jamaican wave —
A paper trinket, hangs from crafty fingers.
Attention, sharpened like a ritual sword,
    Its edge against what's now, what's here,
    Pinpoints your stare.
        You twist and fold
The paper with such wily love,—
        It might have been frail leaflets of strange gold.
Your mood's as still as water. The jewel frog
Sings of your passionate exactness.
                    Blazing, the sword
        Finds its sweet edge in water's tempering cold.

PRAYER

May He Who guides my raw heart to love Him
    Look with forbearance on my love for you.
He is Love; towards earth, from that Love, earth-flames dim,
As, towards shore, sea-hues from horizon's rim
To glass, through ultramarine, turquoise, emerald, dim
    From deepest blue.

PARABOLA

Like a comet you return: regularly,
But rarely. Star-combed, watertumbling hair;
Machete of light.
I crane my neck. An occasion might appear
To wrench the drive-shaft of our galaxy,
Make you wobble back to these skies, then linger here.

But you're a comet, rare,
Slung past my longing, intermittently,
By the universe's wry machinery.

And, no,—
You cannot stop, stuck here,
Nebulous knife.
Sky-puff of ice and dust,
Breath-taking sign, bright comma,
On you must go,
Surely you must,
Swung round in ellipse or parabola.
Rotate. Revolve. Loop. Swirl.— (And I also).

RIDDLE

It is a dream and a riddle,
    From a riddling dream it was torn:
Who is she? She whom you have known all your life,
    Before she was born?

THE AEGEAN, THE CARIBBEAN

(*For Catherine Kingdon*)

If time had sprained its beat and hurled
Praxiteles into the world
Some thirty years ago,
Or so,
And had he known,
As he must have,
The delicate courtesy with which to ask,
(Perhaps encountering you, lover of Greece,
On holiday, emerging from the sea),
He might, most happily, have had you
As model for his Aphrodite of Melos.
So, sketch what changes in stance and profile time
Might then have rendered in that masterpiece.
Expressing you, our sculptor might have lifted
Those lines we know, — fluent, drooped, hip-weighted,—
Elongating the figure so it stood
Tall, erect, on tiptoe,
One steep-arched foot before the other,
A beach-cape warming the swim-suited body,
But kept that kirtle, draped in slipping folds.
Below it in the marble might have been carved
Rings of sea-swirl and eddy around taut insteps;
Hair uncoiling, blown straight back, wind-fanned,
Cupped on the forehead, a contemplative hand,
Tucked in the other a frosty punch or julep,
A sliver of orange split across the rim;
Binoculars slung from one jaunty shoulder,
On the arched spine the head uptilted, searching
For islands crusting the Aegean Sea,
Womb to Aphrodite, to a people's mind.

Poetry has no marble limitations.
Inviting you, I switch his sea to mine.
Wearing the *kente* wefts of Erzulie,
Or, deftly,
A sari,
As tall as the height of the morning star, you arise
From the Caribbean, where poets' and painters' eyes
Split into hot hues the vertical, white sunlight,—
The hues of laughter as it stabs at tribulation,
A people's paradox and mode,—
Mockery, our self-conferred emancipation;
Where, on the main, the Mayan hieroglyphs
Inscribe our western epics, temples march
Up the sky with pyramid profiles, and time ran
To a modern calendar in Yucatan,—
A continent in code;
While, up and down these streets, as yet unborn,
Gathering emblems in its voracious mind,
The staring ghost of Aubrey Williams strode.

EYES

God! What colour are your eyes today, woman?
    What colours were they this last shimmering moment?
        What colours now?

Spectral tremolo,—
Burnt sienna breaks to alizarin, gold-flecked,
To dark wine, soap-bubble-emerald-flecked, to ochre,
                Tawny eyes of the lioness;—
Yours seem to resurrect in you the old, comic powers of
    trance,
    To induce imbalance
        In brain, foot and stomach of each intrepid gazer.

You absolutely will
    Not keep those
        Shot-silk tinctures
Still!

Let me pose that face,
        as pale as cotton,
Against a stretch of Worthing sea,
On a brilliant day, during the erratic
Season of storms.
The sea is changeable too,—
Ultramarine to white lace via lightening blue
And lucent green;
    Lateral washes; water in carnival motion,
                        the white horses,
        The galloping tide.

(I used to think
That wind-slapped, white-horse-rocking sea a field
Of twinkle-coloured, rollicking dancers).

Then ask: Between that sea and those eyes
(No matter how white horses prance)
Which can truly dance the colour-twinkling dance?

1968

I home towards islands, where the sea
Will rinse my restless, bathing eye,
With continental mud now too long blind;
And where, not sour, root-strangling clay,
But loam, friable with humus, crushed shell, sand,
Will bed my crops under the green day;
And O, again, blue sea,
Medicinal essence of earth's rind,
Will cauterize my cloven mind.

IV

DECEMBER 1974: A LAMENT

And the euphorbia,
Snow on its branches, Lord.
Though our sun melts flesh,
The euphorbia whitens.
The year is dying.
My time is dying.
What have I planted, Lord?

And the poinsettia,
Blood stars the hedges, Lord;
Daytime and startime
The red spears cluster.
My year is dying.
My cry dies.
What have I planted, Lord?

And gungu also,
Pods weighting the branches, Lord,
Though Your children are poor.
(Cry thanks for fit food).
My year is dying, dying,
And blood runs thin.
What have I planted, Lord?

I cannot afford
time's waste, fruit-
less sweat, point-
less talk. For time points.
And spears of poinsettia threaten.
Wasting I cannot afford.
Drive me to plant, Lord.

Grand trees I cannot afford.
The quick crops, Lord!
Ambition I cannot afford.
The cash crops, Lord!

AZAN

A minaret coruscates in screaming light.
Suggested doors and windows, of no use,
Declare that mere strict habit is holy.
The crier's voice, in rusty quavers,
Proclaims God great,
Not from that exalted balcony,
But the back of the hall, groundfloor.
Streets ripped by picks and spades,
Dust left to parch and blow
Into our faces, these things show
Where we out-do God: our wastes and deserts
Seem arbitrary and gratuitous.

Seven months ago
Chill seized my sister's heart. She screamed and died.
So I was told.
She was on the green side of twenty-five.

We live under sentence of heart attack.
I also know
Chill caught by the soul, ague in the brain
Can burst a vital vein.
I can't think straight, from ague, chill and fear.
My hand picks burrs from the remnants of my hair.
It is six months since I was called to prayer.

Coughing from dust, I sit in the empty street,
White bones around my feet,
And look up at the minaret
From which there hangs by the heels
The carcass of a man as good as bald.
His youth is contradicted by that pate.

Some pious knife has slit his jugular veins.
Dying spasms have pumped forbidden blood
To quench the deserts of his streets and world.
Billions of red cells, dried now to dead black,
Stir and blow
About with the grit below.
Before my eyes
His wrinkling hide begins to strip and peel.
There he hangs,
Parody of a legal meal.

I can't think straight, from ague, chill and fear.
I sit and overhear
That quavering call to prayer,
As my hand splays the remnants of my hair.
O my God, 'Closer than the jugular vein',
Whose truth includes
Spawning jungle and sterile desert —
I must know, tell me:
Did You require this of them, and of me?

Bismillah-ir-Rahman-ir-Raheem

NEITHER FOG NOR FLIGHT

Midnight. Our sea reflects
Indies of stars
As coral and igneous crusts.
Around each grain of a thought
Condenses and collects
A silence like oil. The rusts
And slags of day have dissolved.
A melody in the head
Caught on a nerve of the tongue
Hints a prayer.

O Breath
That frosts the glass of time
With vanishing stars and dews,
Grant me, as I write,
Cleansed, naked sight,
The hard coin that translates
Your act into image,—
And not a suit of dingy fog,
Nor the word's exhibitionistic flight.
And if such images, tempered, catch
Incredibly a needle of Your Light,
May I be able
With truth to claim —
(As time records Your impulses, O Breath,
As archipelagoes
Are echoed galaxies) —
The sign of equality
Between created thing
And metaphoric name.

'DO NOT SWEAR AT ALL'

Or, if you do,
Account yourself, defaulter, greatly blessed
(Since you must swear, this time you will pay twice,
Once for the oath)
To find the currency
Devalued, or the interest
Compounded and compounded — so you pay
Twice what the books show, on collection day.
For your next oath there'll be
An even greater price.

TRAFFIC JAM IN SICKNESS

dead
tired waiting for your vivacity
to come back from vacation you lounge on
and feel your stalling blood bump inch and squeeze
through straitened traces the highways
of your lean country tightening down from stout
then in then out
then back
round the heart's roundabout

HIMSELF AT LAST

This lawyer's niceties paid for his pleasures,
Maintained two sons through university,
Indulged his fat wife's need for jewels.

In his free time he grew anthurium lilies;
His wife admired them, passers-by begged for them;
All thought him a true artist at his pastime.

Quibbling was an excellent profession
To this dean of small-island mediocrities;
Until one day a swift, sclerotic stroke
Wounded his brain. End of the petty sessions.

His wife has left. His sons have hung *their* shingles.
Now he is what he is, by stern compulsion:
A grower of anthuriums.

Speak praise to heaven for this man's handicaps
Which have stripped him at last down to himself.

RESPITE FOR A BUSINESSMAN

The moneymaker's heart skipped.   Shuddered.   Stopped;
Startling him into awe of an old Truth,
Her arrogance, her starkness. Propped
On the brink of his end, he stared at her
With the rigor mortis of a dimming stare.
The doctors plied their shocking paddles. 'Clear!'
Over his dripping face she flung her hair
And listened for his breath. It looked like love.

Day through the window thinned to twilight. She
Softly withdrew.
Her point was made. His heart
Stuttered back to its beating.
The forehead warmed, after their clammy meeting.
He registered God's mercy.

These days he leaves the city to itself,
Its urgent traffic and its stock exchange,
And potters round his beds of beans and roses,
Clear-headed in his new-found link with her.
(We are the One's, and shall return to Him).
As he becomes increasingly a poet,
Stricken with light, mumbling rounds of prayers,
He notes the calm compliance of butterfly,
Sun-dozing lizard and free-wheeling bird.
We are the One's, and shall return to Him
Who watches us, choosing when we shall die.

TYCOON, POET, SAINT

An island off the main.
Easy to cross to the metropolis
By plane or boat. Nevertheless, an island,
With deep if narrow channel in between.
Radio and television sets relay
News from the mainland marketplace.
An island off the main, which is to say:
Cut off, or not cut off, just as you please.

Thank God for sunshine, rich soil, regular
Abundant rain. From the small farms and orchards
Come grain and butter, vegetables and fruit.
A self-sufficient place. Sufficient too
As home for saint or poet.
But saint and poet have been irrelevant
Since God knows when. Time is progressive.

The prosperous boutiques along the coast
Buzz with the flower-shirted and knock-kneed
Pursuers of swift holiday distraction,
The tycoons from the mainland marketplace.
The beaches shriek with sunlight as it grills
Pallid flesh offerings.

Past the ring of farmland
That feeds, these days, the hotel coast,
The island rises in a stair of crags
To a skull-bald mountain, soundboard for the thunder.
All roads stop short. No one comes here.
(Too few have feet for crags, heads for heights;
Besides, the fun-shops lie the other way).

But scholars talk
Of two that share that igneous, cracked skull,
Their caves on opposite slopes: a saint; a poet.
Both sold their farms when the tycoons started touring;
Both pulled back to the lightning-pelted mountain.
Neither speaks to the other, not from testiness,
But too entranced by the shafts of golden lightning.

Once every month, though never on the same day,
Each scrambles down that runnelled face
And catches boat or plane
For the metropolitan main
To satisfy himself of lightning truth
(Lightning and gold
Are very old)
By proving it against
The expediencies of the marketplace.
And each,
On his way back to the mountain,
Surreptitious among the flowery tycoons,
Stops for a day at the beach.

MANKIND IS ASLEEP

'A modern man lives in sleep, in sleep he is born and in sleep he dies.'

Georges Gurdjieff as quoted by P.D. Ouspensky

Needles of rain.
Pools reconstruct the houses and the trees
Slipping their burden of rain.
The eye, as chances, focuses the world.
Attention pointed to a needle's point,
Needle of melting rain.

So, strictly search
For images now hard now liquefying,
For images of pure fortuitousness.

ZIKR

Is my body becoming a dancer's
Though nobody sees me dancing?

And does my heart begin drumming
When sometimes, by grace, it awakens:

'Allah! Allah!' with awe,
Though my pulse is muffled, normal?

Is my chest a sounding board,
Skin stretched tight over rib-cage?

Does my frame twitch to my heart-beat,
So that I offer foolish explanations?

Have I turned furious drunkard,
Though my speech is clear, step measured?

Do I linger behind Manzoor, the Elated,
Despite workaday destinations?

I shall never again run with the hustlers,
But burn, motionless., imperceptible.

Do I walk through a workaday city?
No. I stand at the harbour, elated.

A landscape of garbage and warehouses?
Abdur-Rahman sees the wide green, gold-flecked.

THE FRIEND

His face is framed in blue light. (Can you see it?)
His tongue speaks truth, brutal like reprimand,
Sweet like correction.
Most of the time he laughs, because he knows
Who runs the world. And they are firmest friends.

But most remarkable of everything:
From total lack of interest in himself,
He has but little inkling of his light,
Being too busy with his Friend. And friends.

786

AHAD

Dearest, I am not,
Save when, as You please,
With Your Hand on my heart,
You set it a-drumming
The code of Your Name.

It is not I
Who make my heart call You.
Drumming Your own Name
On this drum that You made me,
You cause me to be.

I am a shade
Cast by Your shadow.
The sweetest of metres
Is drummed by Your Name.

You give Abdur-Rahman
The heart to call on You,
And that is enough
To make him a poet.

But if I am Yours
It matters not
Whether men call me poet,
Or dimwit, gibbering
The One and Only
Number he knows.

SOUL

Ego must die, so that the soul may be born;
But ego is identical with the soul.
Beloved, resolve in me
Ad-Darqawi's mystery:
You built it into the soul's architecture.

AUTO-BIO

I was born just comfortable. Ethics, art
Were my concerns, at barely twelve years old,
And, yes, a growing love of sea and beach,
Above all, moonlight. The poet blossoming.

Did I grow fruitful? He will judge. For sure,
Much produce fell to earth year after year,
A soggy splattering. Humus my future.
I'm going to the place I came from, Friend.

Now, all I want: bread for my darling ones;
Eyesight unseared by Your exploding suns;
And, yes, wine for my soul,
Drunk from Fariduddin's and Rumi's bowl.

786
IN ONE SWIFT YEAR

In one swift, aching year You summoned home
The prince of friends, then one who walked behind him;
Dearest Manzoor, the pivot of our circle,
Mirror and planet to Your Light (and we
His circling moons, locked by love's gravity
In orbit). And then You called Raouff, sweet-voiced
Reciter of Your Word, who was the map
For our long journey.
And now, let us pray:
Please ask those two, who lean against Your Throne,
To entreat You hold Your Hand above us, Friend,
Still stumbling wayfarers.
For they are slaves to all You bid them do,
And You'll grant anything they beg of You.

SNOWSCAPE WITH SIGNATURE

Against the snow-hill
A rime-clad tree, like branched and crusted crystal.
On mid-branch,
A bird, a brush-stroke
Fluffs at the cold.
At the hill's foot struggles
An ice-arrested stream.
'Whooooo?' asks the wind, rhetorically.
'Wherever you turn, there is a Countenance
That gazes back upon you; there is a signature
On star, and starry snowflake. Whose?' the question
(A frosty, shuddering aria on the wind)
Praises His contrapuntal, terse design.

HIS LIGHT IS RATIONED

(1)

Last night You sundered me
From this dependency,
This body;

Freed me of this flaking rust,
Splintering bone, half-animate dust,
Lodestone to my disgust.

Climbing the painful stair,
Squatting, I sat for prayer,
Remembrance, repair.

Suddenly, muscle and bone
Fell away, heavy, like stone.
Heart-thump alone,

Of all that fleshly curse,
Remained: insistent, terse
Drumming of a verse —

'We are closer to him than his jugular vein.'
Again and ever again
The pulse and refrain!

But, Lord, — why not as yesternight
Do I recite
Tonight?

I am crammed in a prison of rock.
Like rote at my teeth Your Words knock,
Bearing no shock

Of light. Beneficent Lord!
Abdur-Rahman, bound-coolie, your ward,
Complains: 'Love grows hard!'

(2)

From His forbearance
He tips me back to balance,
Calm, self-remonstrance.

Poor eyes, groping for sight:
Most gingerly He pierces your blind night
With rationed light.

THE COMPASS

You blew a pair of bubble gametes; crammed them
With diagrams like winged coils; married them,
And lo! I was. Egg, leech, fingerling, as if in summary
Repeating time's long stages. You hardened
My skeleton. You ribbed and jointed it;
Encased my brain in bone. You fleshed me out; You
    nerved me
For my grand entrance. You tuned my voice
To squall, to gurgle, chuckle, laugh outright;
Steadied my wobbling eyes with focused sight;
Exalted me upon the prongs of choice.

O perfect sweetness! Adult, errant will,
My fuel and compass. Never mind the Hob-Godling
That lurches out of childhood. Rolling-calf,
Bush Beast-Ghost, blood-red-eyed, with a din of chains,
Old Duppy-King, lord of a dripping jungle
Where fears huddle or scurry.
                                        'Me nah 'fraid You!
Me walk where me foot tek me, or me mind.'

I slicked my hair, deciduous now, and grey.
You never turned. It was I who turned away.

One day, abruptly I reversed my feet;
Sought Your direction — so said my conceit.
Anticipator! O, You nudged me, planted
That seed and yearning; yet, from Your Graciousness,
You credit me the sowing.

Did the double prong of choice fuse to one tine
At my decision? No.
There's no contending with Your stern arrest.
To You, like a plain needle, I incline
From Your magnetic virtue, not from mine.

V

WORTHING: MIDNIGHT

Arrest the clockwork of the world
With a rough palm pressed on the sky,
Now that in every wood
Of the fanned, coral-twigged sea,
In the folds of every furled
Cloth of weeds where shy fish stood
Today in sea-strained light,
In the grooved symmetry
Of the waves' footprints on their floor,
And in the pools that lie
For high tide through the reef's door,
In the unwinking sight
Of the moon on its eucharist height,
Beneath the whipping wind
And the stars hung in chains,
In each chamber, on each kind
Sofa or coverlet weed
Every lithe flank, every shell,
Each finned or prickled breed
Wears the camouflage of sleep
And quietly disdains
The possibly waking net
Or curious teeth from the deep.
Now the sky's dial tells
Midnight; while on the shore
The crabs in red and jet
Cool in their nests of sand
Have tucked in legs and eyes,
And each long-necked bird in a core
Of plumage has hidden its head.
It is some hours too late
For any sound of fisherman's wand

Or bargaining by the boat
After the toil of the net
From sun low to sun straight
To dew-time of the sun's bed
And the chill locked out with a coat;
Some hours beyond the time
Of wives on the beach, and girls
With skirts full of shells,—
Some hours beyond the time
Of the faces of my company.
                                        Yet,
Now that the cunning mime
Of branches, as the wind curls
Its whip round sea-grape stems,
And the shadows' gaunt comedy
Play to only my eye;
Now that drunks, fishermen's girls,
All voices, all my friends
Have gone, both tatters and pearls,
There is a pain which quells
That other: my intricate need,
And the coming hymn that I fear
And make without company.
At this hour and anvil I work
Alone, to the wavelets' beat,
To break facility, greed,
Dishonesty's politeness, hate,
All the sins that lurk
In the sly nooks of the heart,
Approaching, I trust, the feat
Of ultimate innocence
And knowledge.

Now I celebrate
In my hymning fool's career
The careful singer's part
For my need and recompense.

IN A CERTAIN GARDEN

(I)

One fruit hung low on that prolific tree.
    A wind nudged by and made the apple shake.
In shifting light the bait glowed luridly.

Silence. The factories of wasp and bee
    Were silent. The convoluted snake,
Beast turned logician, cocked an eye to see.

'You shall know the truth, and the truth shall make you free'.
    It sounded plausible. For their love's sake
They took the advice that did not ask a fee.

(II)

The boy picked sea-grapes by the cross-chopped sea,
    And watched the waves they call white horses break
And stumble, breaking on a fallen tree.

Later, gauche, double-jointed puberty,
    And doubt. Above all, the desire to make
In words something like what his eye could see.

But, impatient with his gaunt virginity,
    He listened to the logic of the snake:
'Lie down with her and call that poetry.'

(III)

The fruit hang low on that prolific tree.
        From too much weight the branches cannot shake.
The logical beast has cocked his eye to see.

Love giving bitter place to treachery.
        Nested in foliage, the restless snake,
Laughing, insists on his belated fee.

Still, caution is the enemy. We break,
        Like the sea's white horses, and make poetry.
Like us, regret and its pointless logic break.

TINKLE FOR A SICK COMEDIAN

Words transmit the jester's thoughts,
    Witty, wise;
Streamlined and feather-tailed, they soar
    Out beyond the flies
        Above the decorated stage
Six yards by four.

His words will cause concerted rage
    In fatuous hearts out there.
The sensible will chuckle, think,
    Brush hands along their hair.
        Meaning's thrill will tickle scalps,
Sharp eyes will blink.

Words transmit the jester's thoughts
    Witty, wise:
Crumbling wisdom spoken on
    A stage of modest size
        By a clown whose leprous flesh is pinned
With chalky, crumbling bone.

FRAGMENT

Knowing oneself, with bleak intensity,
Just a mood short of helpless violence...
A tone, a pitch resembling inspiration...

And then, with temples echoing, to creep
(As inspiration chills to poetry)
The strict way back to equanimity...

'WHEN I DO NOT HAVE BLUE I USE RED'

(for Aubrey Williams and Karl Parboosingh, painters)

'When I do not have blue I use red,' said Picasso.

And when the light is half-spent, you two work by the
half-light,
And in the absence of Talens Van Gogh colours, house
paint will be pressed into service,
And prepared canvas is expensive and snooty, but
hardboard, cut true, will suffice,
And instead of a model, suspicious as to your intentions,
You carry models of all the people of the world,
suspended in the lucid liquor of your minds,
And for the desiccation of thought that passes for
expertise in the academies
You substitute the cunning of your hands, grown nimble
in the presence of discarded refuse;
A stone from the sea imitates the sculpture in your minds,
The accident of a spill of Berger White suggests
Images of stars, comets, the extraversion of spiral galaxies
Unsuspected by Berger's laundered and ironed chief
accountant.
A tree grows out of a daub, as a tree grows out of a seed.
A choreography of trees is resolved out of a quarrel of
angular shapes.
A frog emerges, black, from his city of black and white
buildings,
And hangs from the edge, where the silhouette of board
Discards the reality that recedes behind it.
Though housepaint sticks to houses, it lifts lyrically
from your hardboard,

And the bottle of rum is grateful to look over the
    shoulders of two men
Who carry their vision with a burly, practical grace.
Your hands have been educated by the materials that
    come to hand.

And you know that nothing is eternal, not even the efforts
    of genius.
In 1972 a lunatic claiming to be Christ,
Swinging a sledgehammer, disfigured the face and
    amputated
The left arm of a Michelangelo Madonna.

RAIN OVER ST. AUGUSTINE

The soiled sheet of the plain
Lay stretched in half light.
The rain walked over it on a lot of feet,
Like a *congoree*.
In the grudging light
Hung curds of trees.

I thought of Turner, for I am educated.
It is difficult
To find your idiom
Unclouded by the rain, which nourishes.

LOST IN A SNOWSTORM IN CONNECTICUT

Snowblind. Huddled in a telephone booth.
Outside the four points of the compass blend.
The torque of wind. A paradox of white
Tumultuous laughter at the fact of night.
Blizzard, blizzard, blizzard, blizzard, blend.
There is a smile in the operator's voice:
My accent is enough to brand me lost.
I've wound up nowhere, nowhere without end.

Humouring the climate and myself, I think:
'The equator and the northern latitudes
Run parallel, and on Guyana's main
During December floods
Instead of slanting snow there's slanting rain—
Parallels.'

The problem does not yield to metaphor,
Though I thank my fancy for its frigid joke.

O. Henry drew his neatness to a point.
O. Henry's country. Still
Mere metaphoric neatness makes no point.

ELECTRIC EEL SONG

(*From a play. Gentle, almost inaudible steel pans*).

Ay! me one child! Ay-eeee!
    Ay! me one daughter!
Take out you' foot
    From the black river water!
Haul back you' hand
    Out the slow river water!
Stay 'pon the bank
    Of the cold river water!
    Ay! me one daughter!
        Ay! me one child! Ay-eeee!

Electric eel
    Is the eel in the river
Shadow 'pon the bottom
    Is the eel in the river
Something like you' hand
    Is the eel in the river
Swimming like you' foot
    Is the eel in the river

Ay! me one child! Ay-eeee!
    Ay! me one daughter!
Foot after foot
    Through the black river water!
She can't touch the bottom
    Of the slow river water!
Skirt like umbrella
    In the cold river water!
    Ay! me one daughter!
        Ay! me one child! Ay-eeee!

Electric eel
        Is the eel in the river
Cutlass shape
        Is the eel in the river
Black blade or brown
        Is the eel in the river
Dozing so quiet
        Is the eel in the river

Ay! me one child! Ay-eeee!
        Ay! me one daughter!
Slap of a tail
        Through the black river water.
Shiver like ague
        In the slow river water!
As if she take cramp
        From the cold river water!
Ay! me one daughter!
        Ay! me one child! Ay-eeee!

Electric eel
        Is the eel in the river
No blood, just a thrill,
        Is the eel in the river
Lightning bolt
        Is the eel in the river
And she drown now, she chilly
        Is the eel in the river

Ay! me one daughter!
        Ay! me one child! Ay-eeee!

NOTES

NOTES

Intro:
'Choose my own irons'. The freedom of ordered structure. A poem's force struggles to find and fit its own best external form and order, in this case, the Elizabethan sonnet's clip and punch.

The Madwoman of Papine:
'Duppies' — Ghosts (Jamaican dialect).
'*Oriens ex occidente lux*' — Latin motto of the University of the West Indies. Expanded translation in the next line.
'Rass' — Jamaican/Caribbean term of abuse, equivalent to 'your arse'. Ras Tafari was also the original name of the late Emperor of Ethiopia, Haile Selassie, revered by the Rastafarian movement.

The Mighty Intriguer:
'Mas' — Masque. Carnival costume, band or theme.
'Ballade' — Calypso.

Ham in Exile:
'Canes in arrow' — Sugar canes in blossom, bearing arrowhead-shaped flowers.

'Retour au Pays Natal', 1963:
'Retour au Pays Natal' is the title of a long poem by the Martiniquan poet, Aimé Césaire.
'Demerara' — Guyanese river.

The Self-Fulfilment of Big Rivers:
'Greenheart' — Extremely hard and heavy Guyanese timber, which sinks in water.
'*Stellings*' — Dutch word for wharves.
'Auntieman' — Guyanese word for an effeminate man.

Guyana: Freedom Year:
'Deadly eels' — Electric eels, found in the rivers of South America. They produce an electric charge that can kill most river fish, and can paralyse a child or a small animal, so that it drowns.
'Agouti' — Small, gentle Guyanese mammal.

The Jaguar and the Theorist of Négritude:
'Published in England' — Q: And what about this book of yours? A: Exactly.

The Chord:
'Five/Adopted tongues' — The languages spoken today by the ex-colonized of the Caribbean and Latin America: Spanish, English, French, Portuguese and Dutch.

Going for a Drive:
'Gaulins' — Cattle egrets (Guyanese).

Baakoo:
A baakoo is, more or less, a Guyanese poltergeist, a tiny spirit, in human form, kept deactivated in a corked bottle. If it escapes, all hell breaks loose.

Seasons:
'Lady-of-the-night' — Barbadian shrub. Bears tiny flowers that give off a lovely, heady perfume at night.

The Way Back:
'Jumbie' — Ghost (Guyanese).

Two Galleons:
'Maud Gonne' — Muse to Irish poet W.B. Yeats.

Reign of Terror, 1970: A Nightmare:
This was the time of the 'black power' riots in Trinidad, when the army's loyalties were split, the poor marched in the streets, fighting took place all over the island, and a state of emergency was proclaimed.

The Aegean, The Caribbean:
'*Kente* wefts — *Kente* cloth, a product of West Africa, is hand-woven on machines that are themselves handmade, and dyed in colours of great beauty and brilliance. The slave population of the West Indies was imported from West Africa.

'Erzulie' — Haitian goddess of love.
'Aubrey Williams' — Brilliant Guyana-born artist (1926 - 1990). His work reminds West Indians, Latin Americans and the world that there were developed cultures in the area before Columbus. Many of his symbols grew out of the art of the Maya, Toltec, Aztec, etc.

Eyes:
'Worthing sea' — Worthing is on the south coast of Barbados. Eye-aching whiteness of beach, sea colours that challenge belief.

December 1974: A Lament:
'Euphorbia' — Jamaican shrub that bears clusters of tiny white flowers. It is often planted next to the poinsettia, with its red bracts. Both shrubs flower at the same time — at the end and beginning of the year — and the white and the red set off each other.
'Gungu' — Gungu peas. Congo peas? Jamaican name for what are called 'green peas' in other English-speaking Caribbean countries. Gungu peas bear in the Christmas season.
'Cash crops' — Market-garden crops, such as lettuce, that produce quickly and are quickly sold.

Azan:
The azan is the Muslim call to prayer, uttered five times a day by by the 'muezzin'.
'Parody of a legal meal' — In Islam, for meat to be acceptable as food, the animal must be acceptable (the pig is forbidden), must be in good physical condition, and it must be killed by severing the vessels in the throat, while leaving the spinal cord intact, so that the contractions of the dying animal pump all of the blood out of its body; at the same time, a brief prayer is said.
'Closer than the jugular vein' — in the Holy Qur'an the relationship between God and humankind is described as follows: 'We are nearer to him than his jugular vein'. (50, 16; Yusuf Ali's translation).

Neither Fog nor Flight:
'Bismillah-ir-Rahman-ir-Raheem' — In the Name of God, Most Gracious, Most Merciful.

Respite for a Businessman:
Here, it is poetic logic that represents the Angel of Death as female. 'We are the One's, and shall return to Him' — The Holy Qur'an says: 'To God we belong, and to Him is our return'. (2, 156; Yusuf Ali's translation).

Ahad:
The One and Only; The Unique.
'786' — Equivalent to 'Bismillah-ir-Rahman-ir-Raheem' (see note above: *Neither Fog nor Flight*).

Soul:
Ad-Darqawi — Sufi.

Auto-Bio:
Fariduddin Attar — Sufi writer. Jalaluddin Rumi — brilliant Sufi poet and teacher.

Snowscape With Signature:
'Wherever you turn, there is a Countenance/That gazes back upon you'. The Holy Qur'an, 2, 115: 'Withersoever ye turn, there is the Presence (literally, 'face') of God'. (Yusuf Ali's translation).

His Light is Rationed:
'We are closer to him than his jugular vein'. (See note above: *Azan*).

Rain over St. Augustine:
St. Augustine, a village in Trinidad, is the site of a Catholic monastery, and one of the three campuses of the University of the West Indies.
'Congoree' — Millipede (Trinidadian).
'Turner' — J.M.W., the English artist, famous for atmospheric effects, as of wind, fog, and blowing sea spray.

ABOUT THE AUTHOR

Abdur-Rahman Slade Hopkinson was born in New Amsterdam, Guyana in 1934. His father was a barrister, his mother a nurse. After his father's death, the family settled in Barbados in 1947. In 1952, he won an Open Scholarship to the University College of the West Indies in Jamaica. As an actor he was very active in University theatre; he gained a B.A. and then a Dip. Ed. in 1956.

After that he worked as a teacher, weekly newspaper editor and information officer for the Jamaican Government. In 1962 he and his wife and first child moved to Trinidad where he joined Derek Walcott's Trinidad Theatre Workshop. He was a celebrated Corporal Lestrade in Walcott's *Dream on Monkey Mountain*. He was with the Theatre Workshop until 1970, with an interlude of two years when he taught at the University of Guyana.

He founded the Caribbean Theatre Guild in 1970, but within the next few years kidney failure ended his theatrical career.

In 1977 he moved to Canada as a Vice Consul for Guyana. In 1980 he and his family became Canadian citizens; he has worked as a teacher in Canada.

His poems have been published widely in Caribbean literary journals. Three earlier collections of poetry have appeared: *The Four and Other Poems, The Madwoman of Papine* and *The Friend*. He is the author of two plays: *Sala* and *The Long Vacation*. His short story, 'Marcus Aurelius and the Transatlantic Baakoo' appeared in the *Faber Book of Modern Caribbean Short Stories*.